A STEVENSON SAMPLER

A

STEVENSON SAMPLER

1945–1965

Selected by Alden Whitman

HARPER & ROW, PUBLISHERS,
NEW YORK

Adlai Stevenson was one of those uncommon public men who used a forceful and fluent flow of language to lift Americans above mere immediate goals and to frame their aspirations for dignity, democracy and humanity in words they could remember. His eloquence was not oratorical, and even less was it bombastic appeal to passion; for it was the product of a trained mind fully as sensitive to ideas as to language.

5

Stevenson addressed himself to men's brains, striving to light the way to comprehension of rational man's tremendous capacity to solve his social and political problems in a democratic fashion. Taking thought, Stevenson believed furthermore, was a pragmatic necessity as well as an absolute virtue.

His emphasis was on democracy. He was not afraid of it, nor did he despair of it, even though, as he said, there were times when the people elected for Coca-Cola over champagne. For this he did not berate them, but instead sought to introduce them to a worthier choice by arguing the merits of one over the other. More democracy, a free flow of ideas, Stevenson was convinced, was cure for the ills of twentieth-century America. And to this he dedicated most of his eloquence, using simple words to illuminate, to arouse, to enrich and to inspire the frequently painful processes of thought.

Stevenson's humor was in the Lincoln tradition: its mordancy sought to enlighten as much as to amuse. His humor was the shortest distance between two points, and there was always a point to it. Its task was to reduce the complex to the simple, to make the ponderous light and graspable. Getting

6

people to understand was what Stevenson was about all his mature life.

Everyone has his favorite Stevensonisms; so this is but a sampler, selected principally from *The New York Times,* a selection of those one man likes—and hopes are representative of the man who uttered them.

Alden Whitman

When an American says he loves his country, he
means not only that he loves the New England hills,
the prairies glistening in the sun or the wide rising
plains, the mountains and the seas. He means that he
loves an inner air, an inner light in which freedom
lives and in which a man can draw the breath of self-
respect.

Campaign address, August 27, 1952

9

Democracy cannot be saved by supermen, but only by the unswerving devotion and goodness of millions of little men.

1955

I'm not an old experienced hand at politics. But I am now seasoned enough to have learned that the hardest thing about any political campaign is how to win without proving that you are unworthy of winning.

Fresno, June, 1956

Eggheads, unite! You have nothing to lose but your yolks.

Confronted with the charge that he was an "Egghead," 1952

10

Another lesson that we shall have to learn is that we cannot deal with questions of foreign policy in terms of moral absolutes. Compromise is not immoral or treasonable. It is the objective of negotiation and negotiation is the means of resolving conflict peacefully. But when we negotiate we have to have something to negotiate with as well as for. If rigidity and absolutist attitudes deprive our representatives of anything to negotiate with, then there is nothing they can negotiate for.

Godkin Lectures, Harvard, March, 1954

The only worthy response to danger and failure is a renewed dedication to success; and I trust it will be written of the American people in our time, not that we refused to soil our hands with the imperfections of ourselves and of the world, but that we grew stronger, striving to overcome them.

Speech to American Jewish Committee, New York, May 1, 1963

11

Today . . . we have become so fascinated by the evil conspiracy directed from Moscow that we tend to overlook the massive problems that stare down on us elsewhere. By no means all of our troubles are due to Communism or Russia, and we must take care not to oversimplify or underestimate the complexity and dimensions of our responsibility by attributing all the difficulties of the present to Communism and to failure to solve the Communist threat.

Godkin Lectures, Harvard, March, 1954

There is nothing so fine as to be twenty-one and an American. One is for a fleeting instant—and the other is forever. So live—decently, fearlessly, joyously—and don't forget that in the long run it is not the years in your life but the life in your years that counts!

"If I Were Twenty-one," Coronet, *December, 1955*

12

While I am not in favor of maladjustment, I view this cultivation of neutrality, this breeding of mental neuters, this hostility to eccentricity and controversy with grave misgiving. One looks back with dismay at the possibility of a Shakespeare perfectly adjusted to bourgeois life in Stratford, a Wesley contentedly administering a country parish, George Washington going to London to receive a barony from George III, or Abraham Lincoln prospering in Springfield with nary a concern for the preservation of the crumbling Union.

Commencement address at Smith College, June 7, 1955

Mere awareness of peril has never been known to eliminate it. The world is still very much a pressure cooker, and new ways must be found to release its tensions.

Speech to the Jewish Theological Seminary,
New York, May 23, 1961

13

The first principle of a free society is an untrammeled flow of words in an open forum.

January 19, 1962

A campaign addressed not to men's minds and to their best instincts, but to their passions, emotions and prejudices, is unworthy at best. Now, with the fate of the nation at stake, it is unbearable.

Campaign speech, Chicago, 1952

Nor should we despair. The art of government has grown from its seeds in the tiny city-states of Greece to become the political mode of half the world. So let us dream of a world in which all states, great and small, work together for the peaceful flowering of the republic of man.

Address to Harvard Alumni Association, June 17, 1965

14

There was a time, and it was only yesterday, when the United States could and did stand aloof. In the days of our national youth Washington warned against "entangling alliances," John Adams spoke of that "system of neutrality and impartiality" which was to serve us long and well, and Jefferson enumerated among our blessings that we were "kindly separated by nature and a wide ocean from the exterminating havoc of one quarter of the globe." But those days are gone forever.

Godkin Lectures, Harvard, March, 1954

I say that America has been called to greatness. The summons of the twentieth century is a summons to our vision, to our humanity, to our practicality. If these provide the common purpose of America and Asia, of our joint enterprise, of our progress together, we need have no fear for the future. Because it will belong to free men.

Campaign speech, San Francisco, September 9, 1952

There's an important difference, it seems to me, between Communism as we view it and Communism as some of the Asian peoples view it. When we think of Communism we think of what we are going to lose. When many of the Asiatics think of Communism they think of what they are going to gain—especially if they believe that they have nothing to lose.

Campaign speech, San Francisco, September 9, 1952

I have great faith in the people. As to their wisdom, well, Coca-Cola still outsells champagne. They may make mistakes. They do sometimes. But given time they correct their mistakes—at two- or four-year intervals.

Address to Gridiron Club, Washington, D.C., 1952

The sunrise of our century was bloody. God willing, the sunset will be golden.

Springfield, Missouri, 1950

16

And here let me say something to those abroad who may mistake our present wrangling for weakness. We have always had differences of opinion which have produced all sorts of noises and confusion— especially in campaign years! But it is the kind of noise that, to the inner ear, is the sweet music of free institutions. It is the kind of noise that has produced the harmony of firm purpose whenever our people have been put to the test. The costliest blunders have been made by dictators who did not quite understand the workings of real democracy and who mistook diversity for disunity.

Campaign speech, San Francisco, September 9, 1952

The will to peace cannot be legislated; it must be developed, and can only be developed by organized, patient effort. The laws and institutions of international cooperation have to evolve out of a combination of the common aspirations and experience of the peoples of the world.

London, 1945

17

Let's talk sense to the American people. Let's tell them the truth, that there are no gains without pains, that we are now on the eve of great decisions, not easy decisions, like resistance when you're attacked, but a long, patient, costly struggle which alone can assure triumph over the great enemies of men—war, poverty and tyranny—and the assaults upon human dignity which are the most grievous consequences of each.

Acceptance speech at the Democratic National Convention,
Chicago, 1952

I tell you now that I will never fear to negotiate in good faith with the Soviet Union, for to close the door to the conference rooms is to open a door to war. Man's tragedy has all too often been that he has grown weary in the search for an honorable alternative to war and, in desperate impatience, has turned to violence.

Campaign speech, Hamtramck, Michigan, 1952

As Americans we are accustomed to political bad manners and billingsgate. After a century and a half we have developed some immunity to vilification, abuse and misrepresentation in our domestic public dialogue. If not an ornament to the American tradition it is at least a part of it, and we have learned somehow to give it a rough evaluation and get along surprisingly well in spite of deceit, demagoguery and verbal violence. While rough-and-tumble American political manners have been an interesting curiosity to foreigners for generations, they have had little effect on the rest of the world.

But now the situation has changed with the change in America's position in the world. Everyone is listening attentively to what we say but without even our imperfect capacity to evaluate its significance. The voice of America is not just the government radio but the angry words, defiant proclamations and oratorical attitudes of American politicians and leaders. They may be talking to the folks back home for votes or effect, but what they say echoes and re-echoes around the world. And I can personally testify that what they say is often greeted in deadly seriousness as a reflection of America.

Godkin Lectures, Harvard, March, 1954

19

Long ago we asserted a great principle on this continent: that men are, and of right ought to be, free. Now we are called upon to defend that right against the mightiest forces of evil ever assembled under the sun.

Campaign speech, Chicago, 1952

We are all standing shoulder to shoulder—with a hydrogen bomb ticking in our pockets.

Godkin Lectures, Harvard, March, 1954

If Communism is a problem for the United Nations, so is the United Nations a problem for Communism. The United Nations is a community of tolerance and a community of tolerance is a terrible frustration to the totalitarian mind.

Address at the U.N., June 19, 1962

Diplomacy . . . is not the art of asserting ever more emphatically that attitudes should not be what they clearly are. It is not the repudiation of actuality, but the recognition of actuality, and the use of actuality to advance our national interests.

Godkin Lectures, Harvard, March, 1954

And to the Soviet Union I would say: There are laws of history more profound, more inescapable than the laws dreamed up by Marx and Lenin—laws which belong not to class relationships or stages of economic development, but to the nature and the destiny of man himself. Among these laws is the certainty that war follows when new empires thrust into collapsing ruins of the old. So stay your ambitions . . . do not sabotage the only institution [the U.N.] which offers an alternative to imperialism.

Radio address during the Congo crisis which was under debate at the U.N. on March 2, 1961

Ours is a sad, disillusioned world. Too many people on this blood-soaked, battered globe live in constant fear and dread; fear of hunger and want, dread of oppression and slavery. Poverty, starvation, disease and repression stalk the world, and over us all hangs the menace of war like a gloomy shroud. But everywhere people cling to their hope and their faith in freedom and justice and peace—though fear, anguish, even death are their daily lot.

Springfield, Illinois, 1948

I don't share the concern of some of my contemporaries about student demonstrations. I rather like their involvement in great issues. But if I could offer demonstrators one word of advice I would say that to state goals is easy; to tell us how to get there is not so easy. A moral commitment is hardly meaningful without a practical hope of improving the human condition.

Address to Harvard Alumni Association, June 17, 1965

The first step in learning our new role in world affairs is not one which can be taken by technicians in the State Department, or even by political leaders. It has to be taken by individual Americans, in the privacy of their own homes, hearts and souls. It involves a conscious acceptance of Christian humility —a recognition that we are never going to solve many of the hard problems of the world, but will simply have to learn to live with them, for years and maybe for centuries.

Godkin Lectures, Harvard, March, 1954

In the age-old struggle against tyranny over the bodies and minds and the souls of men we know there can be no respite, no rest, no hesitation, no turning back.

Chicago, 1950

Communism is the corruption of a dream of justice.

Urbana, Illinois, 1951

We are in Southeast Asia to help our friends preserve their own opportunity to be free of imported terror, or alien assassination managed by the North Vietnam Communists based in Hanoï and backed by the Chinese Communists from Peking.

Statement in a U.N. Security Council debate, August 5, 1964

Americans have always assumed, subconsciously, that all problems can be solved; that every story has a happy ending; that the application of enough energy and goodwill can make everything come out right. In view of our history, this assumption is natural enough. As a people we have never encountered any obstacle that we could not overcome. The Pilgrims had a rough first winter, but after that the colony flourished. Valley Forge was followed naturally by Yorktown. Daniel Boone always found his way through the forest. We crossed the Alleghenies and the Mississippi and the Rockies with an impetus that nothing could stop. The wagon trains got through; the Pony Express delivered the mail; in spite of Bull Run and the Copperheads, the Union was somehow preserved. We never came across a river we couldn't bridge, a depression we couldn't overcome, a war we couldn't win. So far, we have never known the tragedy, frustration and sometimes defeat which are ingrained in the memories of all other peoples.

Godkin Lectures, Harvard, March, 1954

I think that government is more than the sum of all the interests; it is the paramount interest, the public interest. It must be the efficient, effective agent of a responsible citizenry, not the shelter of the incompetent and the corrupt. It must be the positive business of all of us, and beneath the dignity of none of us. It must be the honorable calling the founders of a government by the governed meant it to be.

Bloomington, Illinois, 1948

25

What is the lesson of history and of all human experience? What is the primary law of life? You struggle and you survive—you fail to struggle and you perish. The ways of the world are marked with the bones of people who hesitated.

Campaign speech, Chicago, 1952

The ordeal of our times, I have suggested, is a challenge to American maturity and American responsibility. Nowhere is this testing more fundamental than in the field of the free mind. For never has an external threat required more clear-headed analysis, more hard and sober thought and more bold and unterrified vision than the threat we confront today. And yet the very existence of that threat has created strains and tensions, anguish and anxiety, which beat upon the free mind, surround it, torment it and threaten to smother it.

Godkin Lectures, Harvard, March, 1954

26

What power have we to coerce our friends in Europe? What assurance have we that direct action against either Communist giant will not unleash the nuclear war from which we would suffer as much as they? How can we be sure that unlimited support of any authoritarian anti-Communist government may not merely hasten the day when its citizens become Communists as the only means to change?

If total isolationism is no answer, total interventionism is no answer either. In fact, the clear, quick, definable, measurable answers are all ruled out. In this new twilight of power there is no quick path to a convenient light switch.

Address to Harvard Alumni Association, June 17, 1965

I have faith in the people and in their chosen leaders: men of high purpose, goodwill and humble hearts, men quite prepared to stand aside when the time comes and allow even more humble men to take over.

Address to Gridiron Club, Washington, D.C., 1952

I don't believe irresponsible promises are good politics. Promise-peddling and double talk may be expedient and catch some votes from the unwary and innocent, but promises also have a way of coming home to roost.

Gubernatorial campaign speech in Peru, Illinois, 1948

Our objective is not the destruction of Communism by war. Our objective is not the incitement of others to violence. Our objective is not to rectify the boundaries and correct the unnatural divisions that afflict the world by force but by peaceful processes. Our objective is a peace consistent with decency and justice. And our prayer is that history will not say that we led a noble but a lost cause.

Godkin Lectures, Harvard, March, 1954

Unreason and anti-intellectualism abominate thought. Thinking implies disagreement; and disagreement implies nonconformity; and nonconformity implies heresy; and heresy implies disloyalty—so, obviously, thinking must be stopped. But shouting is not a substitute for thinking and reason is not the subversion but the salvation of freedom.

Godkin Lectures, Harvard, March, 1954

When I was a boy I never had much sympathy for a holiday speaker. He was just a kind of interruption between the hot dogs, a fly in the lemonade.

Campaign speech, Flint, Michigan, 1952

Military power without a moral base is always intolerable.

Springfield, Illinois, 1950

29

As to my future: Well, there are those like the man who changed the sign on his car after the election from "Switched to Stevenson" to "Switched, Bothered and Bewildered," who feel that I should devote my classic talents to the welfare of mankind by frequent talking.

Then there is another smaller group who insist that God and/or the election has appointed me the scourge of the Republican Party. And finally there is the much smaller group that feels that it is not wholly unworthy or improper to earn a living. My sons are numbered in the latter group.

Address to Gridiron Club, Washington, D.C., 1952

I cannot agree that it should be the declared public policy of Illinois that a cat visiting a neighbor's yard or crossing the highway is a public nuisance. It is in the nature of cats to do a certain amount of unescorted roaming . . . to escort a cat abroad on a leash is against the nature of the owner. Moreover, cats perform useful service, particularly in the rural areas, in combating rodents—work they necessarily perform alone and without regard for party lines. . . . The problem of the cat versus the bird is as old as time. If we attempt to resolve it by legislation, who knows but what we may be called upon to take sides as well in the age-old problems of dog versus cat, bird versus bird, or even bird versus worm. In my opinion, the State of Illinois and its local governing bodies already have enough to do without trying to control feline delinquency.

Message to Illinois Senate explaining
his refusal to approve a bill that would restrain
the freedom of cats, April 23, 1949

The whole notion of loyalty inquisitions is a natural characteristic of the police state, not of democracy.

Veto of Senate Bill 102, Springfield, Illinois, 1951

The phrase civil rights means a number of concrete things. It means the right to be treated equally before the law. It means the right to equal opportunity for education, employment and decent living conditions. It means that none of these rights shall be denied because of race or color or creed. The history of freedom in our country has been the history of knocking down the barriers to equal rights. One after another they have fallen, and great names in our history record their collapse: the Virginia Statute of Religious Freedom, the Bill of Rights, the Emancipation Proclamation, the Woman's Suffrage Amendment, down to the 1947 Report of the President's Commission on Civil Rights.

Campaign speech, New York, 1952

Our strength stems less from our material and technical attainments as a nation than from our historic record in securing and broadening the rights of our people. From the earliest settlement of this country, America has been a symbol of hope wherever men have aspired to be free and stand erect.

We have learned from the past, and more recently in the bitter experience of two world wars, that today human freedom is indivisible. We have come to know that the basic human rights we cherish are linked with the fate of even the most humble and remote peasant. Whenever fundamental rights are denied, freedom everywhere is threatened, whether it be in far-off Korea or in Cicero, Illinois.

Campaign speech, Springfield, Illinois, 1952

The answer must come from the whole citizen—the whole man. Nobody is just a farmer, or just a farm woman, or just a businessman depending on farmers for his prosperity, or just a worker in a meat-packing plant. The fragmentary man is a myth.

Campaign speech, Fort Dodge, Iowa, 1952

33

Here at the end of the long road, a lot of memories of these crowded weeks flood in upon me.

I remember the night at Dallas, when I spoke to Texans of my views about tidelands oil.

I remember the crowd in Detroit on Labor Day when I said I would be the captive of all the American people and no one else.

I remember the evening in the railroad station at New Haven when I identified a powerful Democratic leader as not my kind of Democrat.

I remember the American Legion convention when I said that those who have served this country must always be Americans first and veterans second, and that our free-enterprise system must include free enterprise for the mind.

I remember the audiences down South listening to what I had to say on the subject of civil rights.

In these and many other cases there were those who pointed to their perils and urged another course. That would have been easy—but I would not feel as good as I do sitting here tonight on election eve.

Looking back, I am content. Win or lose, I have told you the truth as I see it. I have said what I meant and meant what I said. I have not done as well as I should like to have done, but I have done my best, frankly and forthrightly; no man can do more, and you are entitled to no less.

Chicago, November 3, 1952

Every age needs men who will redeem the time by living with a vision of things that are to be.

Alton, Illinois, November 9, 1952

. . . Author, producer and star of Mr. Khrushchev's new play, ''A Funny Thing Happened to Me on the Way to Cuba.''

*Introducing the late President Kennedy
at a banquet in 1962, shortly after the Soviet Union removed
its missiles from Cuba*

35

It is hard for some people to grow old without becoming cynical, but I would say to young people: Listen to the old and the young courteously but be careful who influences you. If you run across those who see no good in the world, who say that everything is going to the dogs and that most people are rascals, don't believe them. But don't reject wisdom from whatever source it may come. Some of your elders have lived a long time, some of them have learned much. The trick is to select the truly wise ones and listen to them.

Chicago, 1949

The identity of the United Nations with our deepest convictions about the nature and destiny of man is a central fact we need to keep in mind as we move through a period of relentless turmoil and travail.

Testimony before a Senate committee considering his appointment as U.S. Chief Delegate to the U.N. on January 11, 1961

Respect for intellectual excellence, the restoration of vigor and discipline to our ideas of study, curricula which aim at strengthening intellectual fiber and stretching the power of young minds, personal commitment and responsibility—these are the preconditions of educational recovery in America today; and, I believe, they have always been the preconditions of happiness and sanity for the human race.

Address to United Parents Association, April 6, 1958

The scientific mastery of our environment has brought us not tranquillity but rather unrest and new fears. Knowledge alone is not enough. It must be leavened with magnanimity before it becomes wisdom.

Godkin Lectures, Harvard, March, 1954

37

The way to solve a community problem is to get together with the neighbors.

The most American thing about America is the free common school system. Here, democracy is at its best. . . .

We do not follow, in America, the jungle doctrine of the survival of the so-called fittest; we follow, rather, the doctrine of fitting as many as possible for survival. From kindergarten to university, in technical schools, agricultural schools, vocational schools, continuation schools, professional schools, evening schools, adult classes and libraries, we open the door of opportunity to all. It should be our purpose to make sure that that door is kept open in all parts of the state for all of the people without discrimination on account of race, creed, color, social condition, geographical location or economic position.

Address to Citizens School Committee, Chicago, 1948

In Washington civilian leadership is most important to the military, because that is where the great bulk of our tax dollars are spent. We must make sure that wastage of our silver is not a privilege of our high brass.

Campaign speech, Indianapolis, 1952

The better you do anything, the more fun and satisfaction there is in it.

One of our hardest tasks—if we hope to conduct a successful foreign policy—is to learn a new habit of thought, a new attitude toward the problems of life itself.

Godkin Lectures, Harvard, March, 1954

Sometimes we get so mired down in the problems of today that we forget the possibilities of tomorrow.

I'm no more in favor of socialism than anybody else, and I particularly dislike things which creep. But, if I don't like "creeping socialism," there's something else I dislike just as much—and that's galloping reaction.

We shall hear no longer the remembered eloquence and wit, the old courage and defiance, the robust serenity of indomitable faith. Our world is thus poorer, our political dialogue is diminished and the sources of public inspiration run more thinly for all of us. There is a lonesome place against the sky.

Memorial service for Winston Churchill,
Washington National Cathedral, January 28, 1965

Friendship is the greatest enrichment that I have found.

At the funeral of his friend,
Lloyd Lewis, Libertyville, Illinois, 1949

The true aim of public welfare is not merely the administration of charity to unfortunate people, but, more basically, the reclamation of minds and bodies and souls, and the restoration of these people to lives of happiness and usefulness.

Jacksonville, Illinois, 1950

Everyone has something to contribute to the welfare of his fellow man. No one is unimportant.

Springfield, Illinois

41

It may be a bitter pill for the complacent, but it is also true that self-government is often more meaningful to the recent immigrants than it is to those who take its blessings for granted. The immigrant comes to our land with homely classic concepts of democracy. He is apt to know what too many of us forget: that no form of government demands such vigilance, such civic virtue, such public spirit and such intelligence. Without the challenge that is presented by the newcomer, complacency, cynicism, disillusion might long since have transformed our society into a stagnant breeding place for totalitarian pests.

Chicago, 1948

I have been much interested in the continued debate raging in the newspapers as to whether I am headed left, center or right. I think it would be more relevant to ask: Is the man moving forward or backward, or is he grounded?

Campaign speech, New York, 1952

I don't like doles. I don't like subsidies. I don't like any interferences with free markets, free men and free enterprise. I like the freedom to succeed or to fail. But I also know that there can be no real freedom without economic justice, social justice, equality of opportunity and a fair chance for every individual to make the most of himself.

Speech to The New York Herald Tribune Forum, 1949

This must be the context of our thinking—the context of human interdependence in the face of the vast new dimensions of our science and our discovery. Just as Europe could never again be the old closed-in community after the voyages of Columbus, we can never again be a squabbling band of nations before the awful majesty of outer space.

Geneva, July 9, 1965

Yesterday when I arrived here President Pusey said, "You know, I've never been quite sure how to pronounce your first name, whether it should be 'Adlay' or 'Adlie.'" I thought afterward of a verse that Mark Twain wrote when he was speaking on a platform with my grandfather in, I think, 1893, and the same subject arose. He wrote it on a menu, and if my recollection is correct it goes as follows:

> Philologists may bray
> But lexicographers say
> That his name is Adlai.
>
> But at political picnics
>   When accents are high
> (Fair Harvards not present)
>   They call him Adlai.

Well, like all politicians, I really don't care what you call me as long as you call me.

Address to Harvard Alumni Association, June 17, 1965

Of course, democracy is not self-executing. We have to make it work, and to make it work we have to understand it. Sober thought and fearless criticism are impossible without critical thinkers and thinking critics. Such persons must be given the opportunity to come together, to see new facts in the light of old principles, to evaluate old principles in the light of new facts, and by deliberation, debate and dialogue to hammer out the consensus that makes democracy possible.

Speech to the Fund for the Republic, New York, January 22, 1963

Oh, what I would really like is just to sit in the shade with a glass of wine in my hands and watch the dancers.

To Eric Sevareid, as reported in
The New York Times,
July 16, 1965

45